IN THE SILHOUETTE
OF YOUR SILENCES

Some of these poems have appeared in New Linear Perspectives (Scotland), Clean Sheets (USA), Salt (USA), The Rusty Nail (USA), 48TH Street Press (Venezuela), Taj Mahal Review (India), The Avalon Literary Review (USA), Primal Urge (USA), Sand (Germany), Arc Magazine, Literary Orphan (USA).

In the Silhouette of Your Silences

Poems

David Groulx

CANADA

Library and Archives Canada Cataloguing in Publication

Groulx, David A., 1969–, author
In the silhouette of your silences / David Groulx.

Poems.
ISBN 978–1–926942–72–8 (pbk.)

I. Title.

PS8563.R76I5 2014   C811'.54   C2014–904752–5

Printed and bound in Canada on 100% recycled paper.

Now Or Never Publishing
#313, 1255 Seymour Street
Vancouver, British Columbia
Canada V6B 0H1

nonpublishing.com
Fighting Words.

We acknowledge the support of the Canada Council
for the Arts for our publishing program.

For J.H.

BEHIND THESE BURLY VIETNAMESE BARS

There is a couch in the alley
we could make love on it
we could touch
and torch the sofa afterward
> *After the word*
> *after the world has forgotten us*
Oh malicious muse
Let me taste
my young Cassandra's
dreams
take this
this broken earth
passing away this earth

WHAT MATTERS

The days fell out of our mouths like stars
struggling against gravity

I give you these prayers
to keep you and hold you

While you are away from me

They are empty like hope
and religion

Under this moon of new frost
they are all I
have to give you

A Strange Wing That Touches

Your wings take me places I do not want to go
your tongues speaks words I do not want to say
you drink what I cannot swallow
lesson this love that I may see
open up my body that my blood will know
your touch

That touches the broken
and the dead

BONE RISING

Trace with your finger to the end of this body
a little while words will follow
a song and the tongue
of this body
stretch your love to me
Rise

Forgive me
I live inside you
this bone that only draws
on your love words

LINES THAT MAKE US HUMAN

We stop in the middle
of this road
and do not know what to say to each other
beneath this moon that has murdered our
creation
now we go
like Cain and
Esau
These promises will not be broken
This suffering will not be in vain
My heart will answer to what isn't said
My mouth will speak to the darkness
and taste what the wind cannot know

ROOM FOR A SMALL PRAYER

In my pocket
I carry a small sky
a bit of a sweet song
a small bone from your body
and a strand of your hair
to protect me
and the scent of
sunlight
that you can find me
where
ever
the swollen surface
of the earth
leads me

PROMISES ONLY THE NIGHT CAN HOLD

Unbutton your blouse
make a pilgrimage to
holy places
the rite of painted lips
heavy with rouge

This is how bodies are built
with fucking
unzip your skirt
while my hands make pilgrimage
to your lips, painted red
with a hunger
not to be alone
We will break promises
to our flesh

Bodies Need This

My body needs this
kind of healing
This pleasure is the only
healing I know
This kind of love
Is the only joy we can know
is the only weapon we have against death

Ending Of Our Season(s)

By the time the plane landed
you were already gone
nobody told me
Afraid I might breakdown alone
Fuck'n breakdown alone uh
I asked to see you anyway
they took me down to the hospital in your old van
the one you were trying to sell
because you knew it was coming
Sooner than I thought
The tape of Tom T. Hall was still playing in the tape deck
the one I made for you
I had forgotten about that
the nurse led me down to the morgue
when we got there
it was cool and dark, *just like the real thing*
There you lay, a cold slab, nothing on but a white sheet
Just sleeping
I leaned over and kissed you
and your whiskers scratched me
just like when I
was a kid

OTHER ROUND DANCES

I wanted to kiss you
half drunk and hoarse-voice
I wanted to kiss you beneath
the wretched neon moon
kisses sweet like
minuteman missiles
on our lips
carry
your muse uttering
moving
desire
Another Round!
and wait
till closing

This Is Love

Your touches are strands
reaching out like light
"This is love" you say
tearing into my flesh
This is delight
>   *This is pure*
>> *This is eternal*

your eyes search into mine
mine are empty, like a corpse
breathing heavy
take me again
Suck the marrow from my bones
>   *The blood from my veins*
>> *The breath from my lungs*

my flesh is open
now
the blood still pouring out
This is love
>   *This is wounds*
>> *This is blessed*

SERVITUDE

Your children don't remember me
I was your secret servant, and not exactly
father material
Fathers need sleep, food and love
I could live without those things
I lived on moonlight, sunrise and the darkness of fury
we were starving for touch and a bloodless autumn

I think about you sometimes now
autumn creeping in my body
and smile
for the memory
of that lovely
mangled summer
with you

Drink With An Old Friend

The shadows grow longer in this life
the vultures begin to gather
we sit
remember the loves we had
the memory that fades
the mind stretches over time
to the songs
and wipe the years away
a spring so distant and furious
now dust collects on these LP collections
only our voices now
can touch our youth
we dance
we remember
our friends
our songs
and the broken bones that led us to
brittle bones
we dance and all that
falls away

TRIP TO OUR MUSEUM

I walked through your museum last night
stared at the kisses you gave me
now behind glass
saw
the diorama displays of love in
the gallery
the pictures of us
that said
Do not touch
the intercom voice came on
THE MUSEUM IS CLOSING

and I left alone

Listening With You Mouth

My fingers *touch* your lips
that, a painted word on my finger tip
the heat heaping
from our bodies
we, our reckless *kisses*
tongues tangled
the aching unbearable
this language we *speak*
only our bodies know

Angels Becoming Earth

The angels buried here
In
Our cemetery
Are
Beneath the dead leaves
And dying grass
Beneath they are
(Broken) breaking
Composting the deepest spring
decomposing changing
into a new hope

Lebretic Magnetism

I have a vision of you
Bending down
Ripe
That lovely part of you
My eyes gaze
At the landscape
flesh
I cannot determine
Your poison
tender
The taste
sweet
The touch
bitter
The danger
satisfying

Some Things Are More Meant To Be Then Others

Calm waters, where do I begin
to see the light
show me a channel to the deep
      A path
hell away
reveal the possibility of light
what songs can you sing running waters?
dancing on the rocks
what thoughts can you say?
God has dammed these hands to move stone
show me moving wisdom
taste my mouth
taste these hands that god has dammed
Show me time that you have crumbled
Show me light that you have broken
and flesh that you have flooded
Oh calm water
I know so little of you

Wishing For A Word

There is only one kiss between us
that hangs like an apple
from a bony branch
its taste like honey
a tickle of tongue
a scratch on skin
draw the blood from my body
and drink
its taste sweet honey
this is flesh
it speaks in touches
one kiss is like fruit on the lips
a pale wish
the flesh yearns

Melody Delilah

You comb my hair
and smell the entrails of lions
and honey
we imagine
smoke cigarettes
and ghosts drift in our faces
ashes of
stares say what we
cannot

What My Muse Says

She tells me things
she tells me these things
we enter into graves as we walk on others
we learn to listen by not listening
and life is a circus
the thread of fate leads to a veil
a heart will vanish but not the heart
that night never ends
we are the flash of a firefly
and God will murder every living thing

Lift Me To Your Garden

Lift me to your garden
guide my drunken steps to your room
tell me the tone of that song you
sing
let me slip in the graces with you
delicate-thin
let me listen to the way you make love
show me the motion
moon light on flowers
this garden
this dangerous garden

Love Making And Life

There are two rock pigeons
Fucking on top of the silo
Vultures fly high over and make a mess of it
Vultures fly high over
Waiting for something to die

WE BECOMES MEMORY

We drink we inhale we swallow
We smile we laugh we stare
through each other
We talk we whisper we sing
We walk we dance we stagger
home
We touch we kiss we fuck
We sleep we rest we dream
of we
We sunlight we moonlight we starlight
We soil we mud we earth
We live we pass through we die
this
memory
alive

Language I Want To Know

When I touch you
this is the language of my hands
fill your mouth with my words
that you cannot speak
taste the tender tongue
that has tasted defeat
climb me with your mouth
. a height that succumbs
to your breasts your thighs
your lips conquer
tomorrow will crumble
in your hands
there is nothing delicate

MOUTH: *To Bodyscape*

Stretch me across your mountains
above your corpse that was written and lost ancient days ago
before the secret grew from your skin
what I told you late at night
stretching over you like sky
crawling around you like water

What is born in your hands
this love
tangled earth and sky
cocks
wings and a clawing

This is what I want for/from
you
that only your hands could speak to tongue
I stretch over you like sky
only our mouths
touch

Love Can Destroy Life

Take this cane from my hand
this rotting eye from my face
this broken tongue from my mouth
hold these hands and all they have done
rise this flesh
take this love
I've stolen from the living
take this knowledge
I've learned from this body
crippled desires
a wasted kiss
Love is not liberty
Touch!
touch what was once devoted
to it

TOMB

The fire still smolders
the ashes growing cool
my black & blue butterfly
away .
Never flutter anymore
I will be closing this tomb
this dead thing
of me and you
forever

In These Small Moments

I have nothing for you except flesh
I light the fire
your red mouth heavy
with chances
We forget our lives
alive
living
In these small moments
we
steal
Our words are meaningless
our
touches
like tentacles
our
kisses
empty

FATHER'S DAY

I stand beside my sunflowers
above me
they are like my children
and I
a proud father

I've kept the ants away all summer
planted them in the sunniest places
watered them when the rain wasn't enough

We take pictures together
me and my Sunflowers
In the bright sunlight
so we can remember
Me, the proud father

Never to share a holiday like
Christmas, Easter or Thanksgiving
all we have is Fathers' Day
and that is enough
it has to be

GLASSES GLISTEN WITH A WORD

We bat poetry around
like it's baseball
drink beer like it's wine
morticians
striking thunder with cigarette smoke
and ashes
words fall like Autumn's leaves
in a wind
restless from lips to glass
sometimes words are empty
like religion
the night passes
a parade of starlight
and dark spaces
sunrise
our words lay broken
across the table

How To Swallow A Small Light

Do not open youth mouth
now
inhale
and hold on to it
like it's the last thing on earth
clutch it with your lungs
let it listen to your
larynx

Do not speak
hold it in

Empty
the sunset
from your throat

Hold on to it
do not speak

If I Could Keep The Fuckin Dogs Out Of The Tiger Lilies

They would be
building words to the bright sky
singing only to the morning sun

The sun would sing back to them
rising from their bed

Sheets of orange and green
stretched out
waving with the breeze

The night would quench
their thirsty voices
with wine

Oh if I could keep
the fuckin dogs out of the Tiger lilies
what celebration
there would be

A Slow Shift In Sound

We speak to each other like
red wine in crystal glasses
we hide crosses
in our mouths

and speak to each other
slow deliberate and delicate

the sounds turn and scatter
like shadows in sunlight

we clink our glasses
and speak no more

OUTSIDE: THIS SCENE

Last known location

: unknown

Known alias

: A needle of gravel roads
: Some of us don't want to be found
: A free feel

Known to frequent beer parlours, poetry readings, strip clubs
And dangerous inspirations

Description—

Known to read vapour trails
And follow fading clouds

Startle deer and
Dream of
saying

something about love

Stares at bodies and smiles
And carries paintings of darkness

Usually spotted
: Always on the outside of this scene

An Autumn Afternoon

We make love beside
the carcass of a moose
that had been poached
the geese V-shaped
building time
out of thin-air
the sun sinking into
that desert called winter
your brown-body against the back-seat
saying you missed me
peeling back skin
rhythms of Autumn
fill our mouths
whisper
to the order of the universe
we are all mouth
hair
and skin
and bone ash

The light ending
the earth moves
on making love
I enter you
and earth moans
the geese over-head
clutching the blue-sky
while we become one heap
of flesh
we make love
we squeeze time
until there is nothing left

The Art Of Urging Language

She sings of her children
oxygen
to the kitchens
in her breasts
a melody
to her chains
that she
spread the last time
naked
her mouth open
her belly swollen
another victim
becoming prison
her children crawl to her
and mouth
the words
mimic the sound
of dragging
language
out of the womb

WHAT APHRODITE SAYS

Don't bring me flowers
they only last a little while
then die
like love
lead me away this trail
show me
the early fall snow
the frost breathing heavy into the boughs
running
the drifts against our bodies
rare
take me down that path
and listen to our masks growing

. . . AND THE EARLY MORNING

Lead me with your tongue
to the places your Muses take
you
from my lips to
my eyes
closed
lead me to the scar on your body
the one that follows the night to the morning
cover your voice in my hair
let my fingers follow the lines of your face
where words begin and end
lead my mouth
with your breath
this moment
tasted
break me
with your love

PRAYER TO A YOUNG LOVER

Touch the surface of the moon
move your body across the constellations
and lick this light with wet
tongue
follow flesh
to an empty December
skin

Lean into the light
again
broken
by bright blue moans

Stretch across the darkness
follows stars
the slender earth
destination

I Make Love To You Like This

We swallow thorns and shadows
my hands grasping
your waist
my hands follow the compass
of my heart
your mouth
covered in dew
my tongue lifting
a flesh-god

My tongue
living
sacrifice

HOW TO KISS A STRANGER

I will give you lessons
at the start
how to do this
And then you go on from there

Take your tongue surrounded
pink
now bright red
floating in your mouth
looking for a direction

From the eyes
words do not know a
secret

The mouth knows
how to make
the shapes of love

Lips tighten and loosen
obey the heart

Words cannot erase this new
knowledge

Eyes close
that they may remember
what it is like
to be loved

FOLLOW ME

I follow you into your hands
led by the choir
of your finger tips

Away from my tomb

Taste the olives
of your Gethsemane
prayers lost
in your mouth

A hunger that
cannot be filled

Follow me
with kisses

Our eyes know
the hunger

Our mouths
Golgotha

Blue Words Following Stares

Empty glasses line-up
in arrow
there seems to be no ending
to them
or words
we say we talk
gardens
weather

and the correct custom of burying tequila
in the throat

We sing we say
to the sea
to the dances in our ashtrays
smoke that drifts away
incense to an unknown God
of silence and dead-ends

I know you as a wife and mother
a god of distant solitude

with the wild parts
cut into slices
left in glasses
with the rind

Beneath The Surface

I swim past you
a hymn in my mouth
and what graces can hide

Beneath water
to the currents
come down
feel this flesh

Touch my skin
make me breath

I'm almost with you
my life is almost
a choir to you

Come touch me
make me breath

That I may sing
about what grace can hide

LONGING, THE ANCIENT NIGHT

Open this flesh
separate away the beginning
the end
end forever
take the music to your secret places
before the beauty disappears
Love is only memory
like this flesh
missing
a moment
a dream barely remembered.

My flesh calls you nightly
searches the surfaces of the night
for flesh
a flash
shimmer
a beginning.

It yearns
scratches at sleep
stretches out
across time and distance

a sigh
a moan
a word.

A body
rising
a silence
touching
a hunger casting spells
become cannibal

this mouth
from this heart.

Sometimes speaks
Sometimes sings

A Slow Dance

Dance slow
My hands
become
disciple of your body
this kind
madness
this stain
lays
another love
Touch you
behind the ear
ahhh
a kiss falls
and shines
touches
only the faithful

FISH-GIRL

You can't be here with me
this fish bowl
belongs to a married man
you'll find love
and it will all end in tragedy
fish girl
I'm damaged goods
I'm off limits
don't speak fish girl
cause this one is spoken for
the flash of a fin
the stare that cannot let go
Fish girl swim away from here
I'm too old for you
I'm turtle spirit
I move slow
I don't wanna see your diary
what your mother said about me
I ain't no fish, girl!
I'm married to the moon
I move time
I dig a hole in the earth
I make room
for new life
I eat fish, girl!
I wait the tide
I don't even measure time
I watch the light
I swim away
I follow Venus
all the Milky way
Is my way
You're not slow
You're not a fish eater
You follow light
like me

I HATE CATS

They say a cat has nine lives
I only have one
to give to you
Purr
I hate cats

Say To The Beast

Come with me to smoke,
bring this beast to my mouth
Say to the beast you are
the arc of an arrow
Only sound can scatter time

Say to the god of bones
You are flesh
Say to the beast of my mouth
You are moonlight skin
and do not listen
when it begins to cry
It is only me

Night School

The first time it happened
I wanted to tell her
that I'm usually harder than this
I wanted to tell her that *I usually last longer than this*
but none of that mattered
because she knew I'd be back
then she'd have time to teach me
a slow
new kind of love

where I put my hands
what I do with my fingers

with my tongue
I learn her body

with her tongue
her hands I learn mine

These lessons we learn
We will not forget

A True Fact Of Love

No one ever falls in love
We fall through it
We endure it
Sometimes we even survive
Tattered
Torn
Lovers die alone
Always

Translation Of Infatuation

I want to hold you
like a drunk holds his last drink
like a heroin addict
holds his dragon needle

I want to kiss you
like the angels kissed Mary
like Jesus kissed
deceiving Judas

Take you to my bed
taste the words on your tongue
touch the rare aching of your body
To know
the rages you have known
To know your bare breasts
turning pink, then red
The longing mouth swelling for
touch

How beautiful
that flesh
that submits to these desires

THE MATINEE OF YOU

The beret in your hair
your silly smile

The way you
bend and twist.

The bracelet
on your wrist.

You blouse bursting
with breasts

From front of the mirror
I long
for
a love scene
: here

(you say): *slowly*

: move

(I say): *forward*

to me.

Show Me My Rouge

You are not Red Riding Hood
and I am not your grandmother

Bring her wine
to me
and watch as these teeth hide my smile

slip into these sheets
Red
your grandmother will
not hear us

Our cruelty is faint
like heartache

Your grandmother will not hear us
Red

this I can promise.

Stretching To The Light You Throw I Dream

Here dead butterflies still flutter
bending the light around
the night

their silhouettes shade
your moon words
I dream

shine

laying against your body
I ache for your light

THANK YOU FOR A WONDERFUL NIGHT MY LOVE

Thank you for a wonderful night my love
a goodbye like this only happens once in a lifetime.
Scratching frost from my windows.
Blood still trickling *blood*
I turn up my collar
to hide the bruises
Emptied of everything
I have.
If goodbyes were like this
I would leave you
every morning
instead of just once.

How Much Of You Can I ?

If you murdered somebody
I'd help you bury the body
and never tell.

If you ever had to shoot it out
with SWAT teams
I'd load the guns
while you got your bead
and never leave

If ever walked away
I'd follow you to the end of
the rainbows
and kill the leprechauns
and give all the gold to you

And if you ever told me to leave
I'd go to the end of the earth
and wait forever for
you to call me back again
you never did
say those words

Becoming Muse

At night she calls me to
her streams
where she dances with the depths
and gives me moonlight to drink

She *tippy toe* along the stones
And catches crayfish on
her tongue

I watch them bounce backwards
into her belly

She invites me to taste
one
"They are free," she says,
"and oh so delicious
despite their ugliness."

The stream swallows my hand
and the cold water fomenting
awaking to my touch

I take a crayfish
from its stone lair
Its small claws pinch my flesh
I do not crush it
"For this is not the way to eat
crayfish."
She says

It swims all the way
down my throat
to my belly

"Mmmm," she says.
"Wonderful, come swim with me my love."

and I tippy toe along the stones
away
and not alone.

I Remember I Used To Make You Laugh

I remember you used to laugh
when I jumped

in the bed

I'd make you giggle
you don't laugh anymore

we sleep alone

What We Are and What I Whisper in Your Ear When We make Love

We are the prayers monks
utter to move mountains
We are the wanting of the air
beneath the wing away butterfly
We are universe
moving away and close together
We are centri
We are the song of walking graces
on every fret of Gallagher's guitars.
Hold me
just not to anything I say.

Angel Of Sunday Leaving

You have left me
for something I cannot see

for something
I cannot understand

and kept my ring

bless your wicked heart

bitch

SIMPLE LIKE LOVE

It snowed the day we fell out of love

it just happened one day
I didn't even know it
exactly like we fell in to it

You came to me
and said
I don't love you any more

it was simple
love is like that

Part Of A Deer Spine

There is an old deer bone in the front yard
part of the spine from a road kill
the coyotes tore the rest away
into the bush

The dog sometimes gnaws on it
sucking out the marrow
sometimes Blue Jays pick at it

The deer doesn't mind

Just A Moment

The beer makes me drowsy
I drift into your eyes
float around your soul

I know I love you at this moment
a moment
a body bending
eyes close

holding only
moment
for
eternity

LOVE AT FIRST SIGHT

When our eyes meet
finally
like predator and prey
although which is which
is yet to tell

A Meal

Our love is devoured until there is nothing left
except maybe my bones
and your tongue

DARKNESS SMILE

I lie hear awake at night
I can no longer sleep
I think about my hands
and all they haven't done

I drink coffee alone and am lonely
in the mornings

I sing and dance
and this does not end it
it is not dust in my eyes
that makes me this way
there is no dust in the darkness

it grows quieter
the heart will speak
what it speaks
and my soul is lonely
for love
it grows dark
and the darkness begins to show its teeth

Night Comes

Love
when will you return to me ?
my love
I've been waiting
like a bird waiting for its love
to return to the nest
waiting
like darkness awaits
the morning light

Where
is your touch my love ?
that one that makes my sleep peaceful
and wakes me rested

Why
does not your velvet voice whisper ?
my love
I can no longer hear your softest of words
in my ear

The sandman comes
to pour his miserable sleep
into my torn veins
I become
his brittle property

I am waiting my love
between the night
and the day
no longer living
but not dead

I become purgatory
my love is waiting
heart be not still

Silence

You've come again my old friend
to see me again tonight
I knew you would
faithful you are
like death

Did you bring the darkness with you?
Ah good
Sit, sit my friend

Wine?

Ah yes wine

We have so little to say to each other
and so much to see of each other
our time together is long
before you escape
before sunlight

like a women
who only wants to be touched
and loved

I know you will not let me sleep
before the wine is gone

My friend
I miss you so little
and not at all

and when I wake I know
you will be gone
like so many before

Searching A Darkness Of You

What is it we search the darkness for?
What it is that draws us to that gaping mouth?

dripping blindness
into the
night field

touching your naked body
like your lover

prayers seem into its heavy layers
building a bridge to whatever light

there may be

We search the darkness
for

We are chaste

We touch its gaping mouth
with our lips
kiss

we pray
together

The light will come

We will be silent

We are torn

apart again

A Revelation About You And Eye

We go with this bottle of red wine
you and eye
to search the stars for an old friend
Ursa Major

A word
we travel to

through us

we stare
and are stared at
by a billion stars
witness
this one kiss

the glistening of the glass

taste the universe
with me

thirst
together

God longs for us.

THE BUSINESS OF MARRIAGE

Let's be pragmatic about this
business like
because
it is business

You may kiss me
but neither of us
want to be kissed

We may stare at each other
but neither us of want
to be stared at

We desire
each other
but we cannot say
and we cannot hurt

Our business is another kind of pain

You may stroke me
with your words
or with your hands

press hard
against me

We crave this wicked
kind of love

soon it will be over my love
soon it will be done my dear

this wretched necessity

This sad business of ours

The Truth About Love

It's cold and raining outside

I want to curl beside you
like a cat
dying of tetanus

from an infected wound

you gave me years ago

What You Never Did Before

You never wore that sexy lingerie for me
it was always those fuckin granny panties
the white ones
that covered your whole arse

Now you bitch about my drinking
saying it too much
and the wrong brand
you never did that before

My mother said you lost a bunch of weight
"Oh she looks really good."
She says
you never lost one fuckin ounce before me

I can see it now
I know it now
I know you leaving me now
and that is all brand new to me

Necessary Amputation

There is so much dead
here for us

and there the moonlight strays
over you voice

still singing

I over here no longer listening
falling
the snow is a verse
we cannot let go

Pale and gnarled
like what love has done to us

severed
our portion pale and bitter

amputated
we went

Why Is It?

What is it between us?
that I cannot understand
come to me woman
show me what it is
show me your stripper boots

Tell me why it is I cannot hear you
when you speak to me
where does my mind go
when I stare at your neck

Why is it I never see you when it's raining?
look sad when you are angry

Why is it I always want to dip my tongue into your mouth?
whenever you open it
I cannot hear
a damn word you
say
to me

Why does the air get thinner around you?
and the earth loses force of gravity?

Why do I go mute?
go on with daydreams

Why is your salvation
so elusive

I can only know one thing
from you
I cannot be saved

As Dark As Flowers In The Moonlight That Sheds

As dark as flowers in the moonlight that sheds
its skin over our naked bodies

plunging into each other
bending backward
leaning forward
tasting the wildness of each other
thick on the tongue
breaking each other
throbbing
thrusting
a forest of limbs
and a river of flesh
tear at
our wet wounds

there is nothing graceful about love

EROSION

We both knew this mountain
would come down
would be shook
till it crumbled
into dust

We both knew its hard fruit would rot
before we got to taste it

at our feet is our mountain
built with laughter, wine and sex
our mountain climbed
and now blowing away
at our feet

No Words Are Said

I come home from work
as the sun is still rising
exhausted
I crawl into bed
and slip my cock into your
sleepy body
I come holding your long black
hair in my mouth
you smile
thank me

we sleep the rest of the afternoon
I miss my own book signing
my publisher is pissed

I fuck you like I never did any of my
wives

When we wake
we fuck again
I feel you come
splashing
against my feet
you moan

I get dressed and go back to work.

Places Ladies And Gentleman

You always thought I was a gentleman
because you always came first

when we fucked in the hotel hallway
when we fucked in the backseat of my car
when we fucked in the bathroom
when we fucked in your boyfriend's bed

I was always a gentleman
and you
a lady

Into A Night A The King George Hotel

I am sitting in the King George hotel
there she calls me to sit

"Come sit beside me my dear."

My dear friend passed out-out on the floor

She asks me to dance, but I do not know how to dance

"Come dance with me my love."

She bends and twists and
my feet walking in gravel

We stare at each other
say nothing to each other

She smiles at me
She buys me a beer

"Come drink with me my love."
I am getting drunk
and led by her beauty
and wiles
in to a night
at the King George Hotel

The Day We Quit Watching The Littlest Hobo

It was about the time
Americans stopped making movies
about Vietnam
but we kept weeping anyway
We played in a band called
the *Hiptipgodfathers*
It was around the time
We thought we'd live forever
We didn't
We discovered television
was too demeaning to the human spirit
a shallow grave to human aspirations
we took our earrings out
and stopped watching
except for Sundays when we
could still watch *The Littlest Hobo*
he spoke to us
about the human condition
and the meaning of life
he was like Jesus
changing lives around him
wherever he went
getting the bad guy
saving the Christians
It was then we thought we were Christians
No
We weren't Christians
We were Hobo watchers
and
he was like sober Jack Kerouac
always traveling the stars
It was then were believed we were beatniks
broke up the band
and began to listen to Chet Baker

We did heroin back then
with Littlest Hobo
we became hobos ourselves
lost our TV
and that's when we quit
watching Littlest Hobo

THE LANGUAGE OF GOODBYE

Which word should we choose
to say goodbye?

A moist syllable between us
We will be through tonight?
a word we search like
though unfaithful
bring me your word
let me drink it
though my thirst unquenchable
goodbye is dripping everywhere

All our words are hollow
We have grown wide
this beauty is scarred
from your tongue

from through this blue
we create
separation of syllables
wet
our love is grown moss
our language has wounded the stars
our nouns are unworthy
of goodbyes

I will not forget
the broken verbs we leave here

Sunshine Swelling Over Morning

I think I wish to kiss you
on your scattered openings
as wide as a field
my favorite sin
always shines in that field
the coffee
the cows coming out of your barn

I think I wish to kiss you
here
now
beneath this sun
here
now
in this field
waking

(A) If I Were Really In Love With You

If I were really in love with you
I would be living
but I am not
in love with you
I thought maybe I was once
maybe
my eyes were closed
but not
am not
in love with you

a demand I will not rise to
a mountain I will not climb
a sea I will not swim in
a desert I will not die in
a forest I will not get lost in
a river I will not drown in
a war I will not fight
(and will not win)
a peace I will not make

a corpse I will bury
a needle I will inject
a rain I will dance in
a(nother) life I will live
a drink I will drink
a smoke I will smoke
the dust disappearing
into the living
I follow

MARIAH

I want to tear off your clothes
Mariah
and make sweaty love to you
while the tourists watch
and take pictures
I want to fuck you while
the moon licks our skin
with its light
in the hotel hallway

I want to stick my fingers
inside you till my knuckles
aching in the morning dew
and all the tourists
can go to hell

What Happens In The Universe Stays In The Universe

I am not Mercury
and you are not the Sun
scorch me with your tongue
make me glow

The only ones who can see us
are the astronomers
and nobody gives a good goddamn
what they see or say anyway

in our champagne room universe

I go around you
I go around
a satellite
a talented measure of energy
waiting to be devoured

WHEN I AM HUNTED BY YOU I WRITE THIS AGAIN

She grows lonesome
for her coke dealer
she doesn't love him
she needs him
like love
I will not see her again
her heart belongs
to her nose
her nose
to a love
that looks like baking powder to me
broken by a razor
I will not kiss her again
she tasted full
in my mouth
a scar
her poison is sweet
in my veins
a curse
on my lips
a rising
these hands will not
touch her
again
this dying
thing

RED WINE OR VIN ROUGE

How could you treat me this way?
this morning
when last night you tasted so full in my mouth
like promise
last night
you were red wine
now you want me to call you *Vin Rouge*
last night we were lewd
now you don't even want to know me
last night we whispered to each other
tell me again
how you conquered kings
corrupted popes
and poets
politicians
and prostitutes

Oh Vin Rouge
love me again this morning
like you did last night
the music
the cigarette smoke
the laughter
the lighting, the rain
Oh you always show me a good time

Love me again *Vin Rouge*
stay
until the rain stops
at least

IN MY BOWING TO YOUR DARKNESS

I find myself
drinking from the glass
where you left our kisses

this hell I taste
leaves my tongue bitter
my lips red

Private Music

Let us start at the beginning
that is sweet
Let us finish at the end
that is always bitter   .

We tumble
we fall
We stumble
we always rise

Over the tables
of people talking, laughing
Across the floor
of people dancing

We make our own music
You and I
a stare
a touch
a word

We leave our prayers against the walls.

I Am Your City

I am your city
whose light you watch
from a distance
from a dark county
I whose sirens you listen for
from a quiet place
I whose heat you feel
from the cool countryside
come to me woman
my urban lust calls
you
my painted ladies wait
my drunken sidewalk
beckons
bring your simple bucolic
charm to me
I am your city
Come, this body calls
you out of the country
Come taste me
the sweat of my shaven brow
rising out of the land
like stiff cock
follow your flesh
I await
I arise before dawn
Sinners love me
and you will too
stay past dusk
Lady
drunk on the sunrise
stay past your bedtime
bring your golden calves
from your pasture

my ravenous heart
gathers a porcine
heap
await my darling
I call my love
you will come
my dear
you will arrive
my love
my love you will suffer

The Dress

I pick up a dress you've left on the bedroom closet floor
like an old love you've left behind
for a new one
A dress that didn't make you look fat
You were fat!
I always thought so
but never said so
like good husbands do
with the hopes of getting laid
even if it was terrible sex
mechanical
predictable
safe

I remember when you bought this dress
brand new
fresh
I waited hours
in the bar
patient
I remember I loved how it looked
on the floor
beside our bed

Now it's just an old dress
I think I'll cut it into
rags to clean up the mess
you've left behind
even if you have
just forgotten it

There Is No Way You Can Hold Me

I could never understand
if you were building a nest?
or a web?

I could never tell if you were building
a beaver dam?
or a fishing weir?

I could never be sure if you
were planting roses?
or poison hemlock?
digging up weeds
or a grave?
in your garden

I couldn't discern
if you were planning a future
with me?
or remembering a past
without me?

There is no way you can hold me
or is there?

Beneath Your Moon I Say To The Beast

If I move
then you should move too
and if I wave
you should wave too
if you wave first
I will wave too
If you wink
I will wink
a breeze from
you to me
and to you

if you touch me
I will touch you

Touch me

move
connect
move
connect

see

see
me

this is human

You Leaving with the Circus

You've packed all your feet and all
your eyeballs
the smell of your nose
and the sound of your ears
now you've put away your
looks and your stares

Took your woke and worn
you've packed away your pretty things
and your ugly things
you've put away your tooth and your tongue
you're dead and wounded
you've put away
with all you remember
and forgot
you're taking your escapades
and affairs
away

You're taking your walk and your run
your come and your came
your fingers and your hands
storing away your laughter and your crying
your snoring and your sighing
gathering your riches and your rags
your elbows and your knees
your lips and your tongue
your fish and your frogs
folding you heartaches
and joy
you put away

Your pumpkins and your jack-o-lanterns
your poppies and jack rabbits
taking your stairs
your ups and your downs
your smiles and your frowns
packing up your tent
and your elephant
the circus
is over
the clown
you leave
behind